Selma Dimitrijevic

DR FRANKENSTEIN

Based on the novel 'Frankenstein'
by Mary Wollstonecraft Shelley

OBERON BOOKS
LONDON

WWW.OBERONBOOKS.COM

First published in 2017 by Oberon Books Ltd
521 Caledonian Road, London N7 9RH
Tel: +44 (0) 20 7607 3637 / Fax: +44 (0) 20 7607 3629
e-mail: info@oberonbooks.com
www.oberonbooks.com

A catalogue record for this book is available from the British Library.

PB ISBN: 9781786821256
E ISBN: 9781786821263

Cover design by James Illman

To Lorne Campbell, for making things happen.

Characters

DR VICTORIA FRANKENSTEIN, daughter of
Alphonse and Caroline Frankenstein,

CREATURE,

HENRY CLERVAL, family friend, childhood
friend of Victoria and Elizabeth,

ELIZABETH LAVENZA FRANKENSTEIN,
adopted daughter of Alphonse and Caroline
Frankenstein,

JUSTINE MORITZ, living with the Frankenstein
family, looking after young William,

FATHER, Alphonse Frankenstein,

MARY, the maid.

ACT I – 1831

ACT II – 1832

ACT I

1831. England.

VICTORIA is standing behind a long table. On the table is the body of a young woman, naked but for a white sheet covering her from toes to her bare chest.

VICTORIA: Gentlemen. Colleagues.

Today I will talk about who we are beneath the surface.

I will start with the functional unit of the most complex structure on this earth.

The brain.

It weighs only three pounds, yet it has the ability to conceive of the universe, and every single one of us in it.

Think about that for a moment.

Really think about that.

–

A mass of cells can do that.

–

It can get angry. Hopeful. Revengeful. Or feel a number of other emotions.

It can remember.

It can understand.

It can invent.

A mass of cells.

Imagine it.

The young woman lying on the table SNEEZES LOUDLY and sits up.

VICTORIA: Justine!

JUSTINE: It's freezing!

VICTORIA: I really need you to be dead.

JUSTINE: I was dead.

VICTORIA: The dead don't sneeze.

JUSTINE: And how do you know that?

VICTORIA: Through observation. Now, please. Lie down.

JUSTINE: But I'm bored.

She lies down anyway.

JUSTINE: Can I put my socks on?

VICTORIA: No.

VICTORIA focuses again.

VICTORIA: A mass of cells.
Imagine it.

ELIZABETH comes in.

ELIZABETH: Victoria!

VICTORIA: What (now)?

ELIZABETH: What on earth is going on?

VICTORIA: I'm in the middle of something.

ELIZABETH: Of what exactly?

JUSTINE: Her anatomy lecture.

ELIZABETH: This is not a place for that kind of thing.

VICTORIA: I am giving a lecture, and I need to be ready.

ELIZABETH: And what, you'll be talking about Justine?

VICTORIA: Don't be ridiculous. I'll be talking about the brain.

ELIZABETH: You have about five minutes before Father
               comes home and sees what you have done to
               the room.

JUSTINE jumps off the table.

JUSTINE: He's going to kill us.

VICTORIA: Tell him you were out with William, and I
               did all this.

JUSTINE: I can't lie to him.

VICTORIA: Of course you can, we all do.

ELIZABETH: We certainly do not.

ELIZABETH is taking sheets off the table.

VICTORIA: Careful.

VICTORIA is still making notes.

ELIZABETH: Now these will have to be washed all over
               again.

VICTORIA: What kind of mood is he in tonight?

JUSTINE: I can take the sheets. It's not a problem.

ELIZABETH: That is very kind of you, Justine, but Victoria
               is perfectly capable of taking them herself.
               Thank you.

ELIZABETH thrusts the sheets into VICTORIA's hands.

VICTORIA: Elizabeth?

ELIZABETH: He is in a foul mood.

VICTORIA: What is it now?

JUSTINE: Here, let me.

*JUSTINE takes the sheets off the table. VICTORIA wouldn't know
what to do with them anyway.*

ELIZABETH: You really don't know?

VICTORIA: How would I know?

ELIZABETH: Ah, God bless.

VICTORIA:	'God' you say? Now, which God would that be?
ELIZABETH:	Not tonight.
VICTORIA:	Is it the one that demands we remove all knowledge in order to make room for belief?
ELIZABETH:	I am not in the mood.
VICTORIA:	It is a simple question.

MARY comes in.

MARY:	Mr Clerval is here.
ELIZABETH:	Show him in, will you Mary.
MARY:	Of course, Miss Lavenza.

MARY leaves.

JUSTINE:	I will make sure these get washed.
ELIZABETH:	Thank you, Justine.
JUSTINE:	And William will want to say good night, before he goes to sleep.
VICTORIA:	I'll be there in a minute.

JUSTINE leaves, VICTORIA keeps editing her lecture.

MARY shows HENRY in.

HENRY:	Elizabeth.
ELIZABETH:	Henry.

VICTORIA has a question for HENRY:

VICTORIA:	Would you say that the 'brain has the ability to conceive of the universe' or 'imagine the universe'?
HENRY:	What's that for?
VICTORIA:	My lecture.
HENRY:	It really depends what you want to say.
VICTORIA:	Ideally, both of those things.

HENRY sits next to her.

HENRY: Do you want to read me what you have so
             far?

VICTORIA: Excellent.

ELIZABETH: And we'd all be delighted to hear it.
             After dinner.

HENRY: Of course.

ELIZABETH: Are you going to see William?

VICTORIA: Yes.

ELIZABETH: When?

VICTORIA: Oh, fine.

VICTORIA closes her notebooks.

VICTORIA: Can you please not touch any of these?

ELIZABETH: Fine.

VICTORIA: You won't?

ELIZABETH: I won't.

*As soon as she leaves, ELIZABETH gets up to tidy, but HENRY
interrupts.*

HENRY: How about a drink?

She knows what he is doing, but lets him.

ELIZABETH: Whiskey?

HENRY: Perfect. Thank you.

She is pouring him a glass.

ELIZABETH: I swear, the closer it gets to her leaving, the
             more difficult she gets.

HENRY: You will still miss her, once she's gone.

ELIZABETH: The whole University business is, if you ask
             me, complete waste of time and money.

HENRY: I don't know. She seems happy.

ELIZABETH: And what's that got to do with it?

HENRY: *(Takes the drink.)* Thank you.

ELIZABETH: University is not there to make you happy.

HENRY: She is learning. That must be exciting.

ELIZABETH: Yes, I am sure she is.

HENRY: But ...

ELIZABETH: But what's the point of knowing how to be a doctor, if you'll never be allowed to be one.

JUSTINE comes back in.

ELIZABETH: *(To JUSTINE.)* Could you please put these away. You'll know how she likes them.

JUSTINE: I think she likes them not put away.

ELIZABETH: Well, that's a shame, isn't it.

JUSTINE: I'll just put them to the side.

VICTORIA comes back in. Sees JUSTINE who shrugs. She doesn't have the power to say no in this house. VICTORIA is ready to argue with ELIZABETH, but HENRY interrupts again.

HENRY: How's William?

VICTORIA: Reading.

HENRY: Excellent. A drink?

VICTORIA: Yes. Fine.

HENRY is pouring her a glass.

VICTORIA: So, Henry. When are you going to join me?

ELIZABETH: Victoria.

VICTORIA: What?

HENRY: It is not that easy.

VICTORIA: You have no interest in running the factory, we both know that. Tell that to your Father, and come to the University. They would be lucky to have you, you know that don't you?

HENRY: Maybe it's just not my fate.

VICTORIA: Nonsense. There is no such thing as fate.

JUSTINE: Victoria!

	You can't say that.
VICTORIA:	It's true though.
ELIZABETH:	It's true "in your opinion".
VICTORIA:	Believing in fate is simply not taking responsibility for what happens next.
HENRY:	He can't imagine anyone else taking over. It's our name above the door.
VICTORIA:	I've seen men do much more demanding jobs than change a name-board over a door.

MARY comes back.

ELIZABETH:	Yes, Mary.
MARY:	Dinner is ready.
VICTORIA:	Thank you.
ELIZABETH:	Will Father be joining us soon?
MARY:	He is on his way down.
ELIZABETH:	*(To VICTORIA.)* Will you be kind to him tonight, please.
VICTORIA:	Why do you always say things like that?
ELIZABETH:	Just be nice to him. All right?
VICTORIA:	Did you ask him to be nice to me? You know what he is like.
ELIZABETH:	He is just worried. Once you leave, you are all on your own.
VICTORIA:	I'm surrounded by like-minded people. I am fine.
ELIZABETH:	You are surrounded by men.
VICTORIA:	Students, Elizabeth. Just like me.
JUSTINE:	I think he should be very proud that you are at the University. I keep telling everyone about it.

VICTORIA: Well, thank you, Justine. That's very kind of you.

FATHER steps in from the hall.

FATHER: It smells wonderful, Mary. Thank you.

MARY: It will be ready when you are.

MARY leaves.

FATHER: Is William asleep?

JUSTINE: Yes. Sound asleep.

FATHER: Good.

ELIZABETH: He's had a long day.

FATHER: Henry.

HENRY: Dr Frankenstein.

FATHER: Have a seat, Henry.

HENRY: Thank you.

I'm sorry I missed William, he always makes me laugh.

FATHER: Yes. He likes you.

JUSTINE: We got drenched today. It was very exciting.

FATHER: Yes, he was telling me earlier. He said you saw – a ghost.

JUSTINE: It was just a tree.

FATHER: That boy has his mother's imagination.

JUSTINE: It got hit by lightning, and it had this huge hole in the trunk. When the wind blew it made a howling noise. Made it sound like a ghost.

ELIZABETH: Were you frightened?

JUSTINE: I knew it wasn't a real ghost

HENRY: You do know what it is don't you?

JUSTINE: What?

ELIZABETH:	Henry …
HENRY:	It's the devil leaving his sign.
JUSTINE:	No it isn't.
HENRY:	*…The speedy gleams the darkness swallow'd;* *Loud, deep, and long the thunder bellow'd;* *That night a child might understand* *The De'il had business on his hand.*
ELIZABETH:	Oh, stop it.
JUSTINE:	Its' true. Its bad luck, finding a tree hit by lightning.
VICTORIA:	Just a natural occurrence.
JUSTINE:	I heard it means there will be a funeral.
VICTORIA:	It's just electricity, Justine. Small particles of ice collide in the clouds, and create static electricity. Similar particles are created in a tree, and when the two meet, there is lightning. It really is as simple as that.
FATHER:	Your sister might have not learned how to run the house, but she learned what causes lightning. The more expensive education is, the less useful it seems to be.
JUSTINE:	Can you imagine being hit by lightning?
ELIZABETH:	Do you think you would survive?
HENRY:	I heard some people do.
JUSTINE:	I wouldn't like to. To be hit by lightning. Would you?
VICTORIA:	It would be interesting.
FATHER:	All right, enough now. You are being ridiculous.
VICTORIA:	I was just saying it would be interesting. I didn't say I was actually going to attempt it.

FATHER: I said, enough.

VICTORIA: It is called a 'thought experiment', Father. That means it's theoretical.

FATHER: Have you ever seen anyone after they have been hit by lightning?

VICTORIA: No.

FATHER: Or after they have been trampled by a horse?

VICTORIA: No.

FATHER: No. Exactly. There is nothing theoretical or funny about it.

VICTORIA: Just because I'm not interested in treating injuries, doesn't mean I'm not interested in understanding them.

ELIZABETH: She is studying the science of the brain.

FATHER: No. No. Let her tell me.

I'm paying for it, so I assume I have the right to know.

VICTORIA: You can stop the payments any time you want.

FATHER: I made a promise to your Mother.

VICTORIA: Well, as she is dead, she's not very likely to find out. Is she?

FATHER: –

MARY comes in.

MARY: Dinner is served.

ELIZABETH: Thank you, Mary.

MARY keeps the doors open for them.

FATHER: Henry. Would you join me in the dining room?

HENRY: Of course.

HENRY and FATHER leave. JUSTINE just after them.

ELIZABETH: Tell me, do you have to?

VICTORIA: I think I do.

(ELIZABETH: Of course.)

ELIZABETH should have known better than to ask.

2

VICTORIA: Mary?

MARY: Yes, dear.

VICTORIA: Do you believe in God?

MARY: I do.

VICTORIA: How come?

MARY: I don't know.

                That is what my mother did, and her mother.
                And I suppose her mother as well.

VICTORIA: And do you enjoy it?

MARY: –

                I do. Yes.

VICTORIA: Why do you think that is?

MARY: I have someone to talk to. Someone to come
                back to.

VICTORIA: And do you believe God created human
                beings?

MARY: I do. Yes.

                Do you?

VICTORIA: No.

MARY: What do you believe?

VICTORIA: I believe human beings created God.

MARY: That sounds like something your mother would say.

VICTORIA: Tell me about her.

MARY: What would you like to know?

VICTORIA: What was she like? As a woman ... as a person?

MARY: She was smart. Like you.

VICTORIA: What else. What did she like?

MARY: Horses. And riding. Books. She loved her books. Walks with your Father.

VICTORIA: What else?

MARY: Being at home. With you. And Elizabeth. And William.

VICTORIA: She never really met him.

MARY: No, I suppose, not.

VICTORIA: Do you think ... if she knew she was going to die. Do you think she would have had him anyway?

MARY: I don't know.

What do you think?

VICTORIA: Yes.

I think she would.

3

Germany. Ingolstadt. Several months later.

VICTORIA's HOUSE on University grounds. The place has been transformed into a working lab.

VICTORIA is on her own. She is used to it.

On the table, there is a small cage with some straw and a tiny RABBIT in it.

Next to it is a metal bath full of ice and water.

She carefully lifts the RABBIT out of its cage.

VICTORIA: Hello.

She takes him to the metal bath.

VICTORIA: There we go.

She puts the RABBIT in the bath and holds it under water. Its kicking as it drowns.

There is a knock on the door. She doesn't hear it.

VICTORIA is holding the RABBIT with both hands.

There's a knock again. Louder.

The doors open and HENRY peeks in.

HENRY: Hello?

HENRY is standing at the door not sure about what he is seeing.

HENRY: Victoria?

She can't hear him.

HENRY: Victoria!

She sees him, without letting go of the RABBIT.

VICTORIA: Henry!

              Come in. Come in.

The RABBIT is still struggling, less as the time passes.

VICTORIA: Wait a minute.

HENRY: What is going on?

VICTORIA: Just wait.

She holds the RABBIT under water. There is less and less motion. She keeps an eye on the clock. When the RABBIT stops kicking, she gently secures it and puts the lid on.

She checks the time and makes a note.

VICTORIA: Hello.

She hugs him.

HENRY: Hello.

VICTORIA: What are you doing here?

HENRY: I've come to see you.

VICTORIA: All the way from home?

HENRY: Yes.

VICTORIA: *(She thinks about it for a moment.)* That's
              wonderful.

HENRY takes in her and her surroundings. She can't really stop with the experiment.

HENRY: What's going on?

VICTORIA: I'm in the middle of something.

HENRY: Are you all right?

VICTORIA: I've been up for a while, that's all.

HENRY: Have you?

VICTORIA: Yes. Have a seat.

HENRY: I'm fine.

VICTORIA goes back to her work bench, simultaneously talking to HENRY and preparing for the next stage of the experiment.

VICTORIA: How about hot drink?

              How about coffee?

HENRY: Yes, please.

VICTORIA: Mary!

There is no response. VICTORIA checks the metal bath, makes a few notes.

VICTORIA: You didn't come all the way here just to see me, did you?

HENRY: Of course I did.

VICTORIA: Someone's died. Is it Father?

HENRY: No one.

VICTORIA: You know you can tell me.

HENRY: No one is dead. Trust me. Everyone is just fine. They send their love.

VICTORIA: Mary!

There is no response.

During the conversation VICTORIA takes the RABBIT out of the metal bath, transfers it to a deep tray and places it on a slab of ice.

HENRY: I've come to see you.
              To see how you are doing, what you are doing?

VICTORIA: You must've been traveling for days.

HENRY is not sure what she is doing or if he should be there while she is doing it. VICTORIA has made a small cut and is bleeding the RABBIT while injecting a formaldehyde-based solution to replace the blood.

HENRY: Would you like me / to wait outside?

VICTORIA: / Don't be ridiculous.

HENRY: Is that ...

VICTORIA: It's just a rabbit.

HENRY: You know, your Father is worried about you.

VICTORIA: Why?

HENRY: You haven't written in months.

VICTORIA: Of course I have.

HENRY: When?

VICTORIA:	I'm sure I did.
	I sent at least one letter in … May?
HENRY:	It's September now.
VICTORIA:	Oh. I'm busy. Henry. With the work, and the lectures.
HENRY:	They would just like a letter. That's all. From time to time. So they know you are all right.
VICTORIA:	Fine. I'll write.

She finds another piece of paper.

VICTORIA:	What would they like me to say?
HENRY:	I don't know.
VICTORIA:	–
HENRY:	You should ask about their health? Tell them how you are.
VICTORIA:	But they are all well?
HENRY:	Yes.
VICTORIA:	Then why do I have to ask?
HENRY:	So you can tell them how you are?
VICTORIA:	Oh, Henry, these things just take so much time … hold on.

She checks the time and writes something down. While she is writing, she continues talking to HENRY.

VICTORIA:	Can you not just tell them everything is fine?
HENRY:	Is it?
VICTORIA:	Yes. I'm fine.

VICTORIA has finished draining the RABBIT. She dries him with a cloth and places him into another metal bath, with a glass top.

HENRY:	Where did you get that?
VICTORIA:	The rabbit?
HENRY:	No. The ice.

VICTORIA: Just one of the advantages of being at the University.

HENRY touches the ice where the RABBIT was a moment ago.

VICTORIA: I was talking to one of the doctors a while ago, to Professor Waldman. He said something, he said something very interesting, he said *'if only we could stop time, to give us a moment to think, a moment to act'.*

It's a revolutionary thought, Henry, *'if only we could stop time'.*

HENRY: Well – we can't.

VICTORIA: Have a look.

She shows him the metal bath, one where the RABBIT is. He looks through the glass top.

HENRY: It's dead.

VICTORIA: Yes.

HENRY: –

VICTORIA: For now.

HENRY: What do you mean 'for now'?

VICTORIA: That's what I've been working on. Death.

HENRY: I'm sorry?

VICTORIA: There's a very thin line, Henry, between being dead and being alive.

I have been looking into how the two states exist together, how they join.

I think I can find out what is it that keeps us alive.

HENRY: –

Good.

VICTORIA: Don't patronise me Henry. It doesn't suit you.

HENRY: I'm sorry. It's all just a bit …

VICTORIA:	Too much?
HENRY:	Yes.
VICTORIA:	Apology accepted. Coffee?
	Mary!
HENRY:	Do you have someone living with you?
VICTORIA:	*(She realises.)* No. Of course not.
	Mary is at home. Isn't she?
HENRY:	Yes.
VICTORIA:	Of course she is.

VICTORIA goes to the other bench where very similar equipment is used to make coffee.

HENRY steps away from the RABBIT. He takes his coat off, he is having a look around.

| VICTORIA: | Don't touch anything. |
| HENRY: | (Don't worry.) I wasn't planning to. |

The clock on the table goes off. VICTORIA comes back to the RABBIT.

| VICTORIA: | Excuse me. |

She checks the time, checks the RABBIT, takes the electrodes and waits.

| HENRY: | What's that / for? |
| VICTORIA: | / Shhhh. |

She is standing motionless, waiting, looking at the clock.

When the time is right, she turns on the electrodes and electrocutes the RABBIT.

| HENRY: | What did you do to it? |
| VICTORIA: | You'll see in a minute. |

VICTORIA goes back to the coffee.

| VICTORIA: | Sugar? |
| HENRY: | Yes, please. |

HENRY is not sure if she's completely lost her mind.

He doesn't want to go anywhere near the tub.

There is a curtain covering one end of the room.

As HENRY *is wondering around the room, he ends up near the curtain, and peeks behind.*

HENRY: Jesus Christ! What's that?

She brings them two cups of coffee.

VICTORIA: Oh.

A man. Well ... a body, to be more precise.

HENRY: What is it doing here?

VICTORIA: It's my research. At the hospital, there's always someone coming in and out.

It's just easier this way.

HENRY: He is dead.

VICTORIA: Yes.

HENRY: So how did he get here?

VICTORIA: Does it matter?

HENRY: Of course it does.

VICTORIA: I have couple of men, friends, let's say, people who have been recommended to me. I buy their dinner from time to time, they help me with things.

Things like this.

She is keeping an eye on the RABBIT.

HENRY: Have they ... killed him?

VICTORIA: Of course not. He was already dead. He drowned.

HENRY: What about his family?

VICTORIA: If he had any, they didn't care to make it known. He would have been buried at the public expense, so there's really no harm in him being here instead.

HENRY *is observing the body from a far.*

HENRY: And what do you do with it now?

VICTORIA: You see, once a person has died, there might be a small window of time during which it is possible – through keeping them extremely cold – to halt the process of decomposition.

HENRY: Why would you do that?

VICTORIA: So I can then bring them back to life.

HENRY: –

              No.

VICTORIA: Actually, yes. I have developed a medical infusion, an elixir if you like, extracted human hormone and a mixture of formaldehyde, glutaraldehyde, methyl alcohol, ethanol and water, which can – if given at the right time, under the right circumstances – do exactly that.

              Stop the time.

HENRY: –

VICTORIA: –

HENRY: So you can bring people back to life?

VICTORIA: Well, not yet. Not people. But soon.

HENRY: Victoria / ...

VICTORIA: Do you want to touch him?

HENRY: No!

VICTORIA: Why not?

HENRY: I don't know. He looks strange.

              He looks very ... cold.

VICTORIA: The blood's been drained. There's nothing to keep him warm.

HENRY: –

VICTORIA: Go on. He is just a person. Like you and I. Just cold.

Go on.

HENRY goes closer. He is next to the body. Just as he is about to touch it, there is banging from the bunny tub. He jumps away.

HENRY: What the hell is that?

VICTORIA: Come.

VICTORIA opens the tub where the dead RABBIT was. She reaches in and takes it. He is alive.

VICTORIA: Remember him?

HENRY: This is insane.

VICTORIA is holding a healthy looking RABBIT. Very much alive.

VICTORIA: Henry. This is Prometheus.

HENRY: No.

VICTORIA: Say hi. Hi Prometheus.

HENRY: How?

                         –

                    How?

VICTORIA: Profound challenges demand profound
                    solutions.

HENRY: *(Re the body.)* Is he also going to …

VICTORIA: No. I thought he would. But he didn't.

                    And I don't know why.

HENRY: Do you have anything stronger?

VICTORIA: Whiskey?

HENRY: Yes. Yes, please.

VICTORIA looks at the shelf. Just empty bottles.

VICTORIA: No. There's none.

HENRY: Can we go out?

VICTORIA: Do you want to hold him?

HENRY: No.

VICTORIA: Go on.

HENRY:	No.
VICTORIA:	Oh, it's so good to see you Henry.
HENRY:	Look. I think I need a moment to … to get some air. To be outside.
VICTORIA:	Hold on.

She puts the RABBIT back into his cage. HENRY goes closer.

HENRY:	Is he really … was he dead? And now he is alive?
VICTORIA:	Yes. You could say that.
	Although how much this 'he' is still the old 'he', I wouldn't want to guarantee.
HENRY:	How can you tell?
VICTORIA:	They don't remember things, where to find food, how to get out. I can't be sure, but I don't think they remember me either.
HENRY:	That's good. Otherwise they might remember it was you who killed them.
VICTORIA:	And brought them back to life.
HENRY:	Can you please lock it up?
VICTORIA:	'Him'.
HENRY:	Lock him up, lock all this up, and – can we please get out of here.

VICTORIA locks the RABBIT, says bye, and takes her coat.

VICTORIA:	Shall we?
HENRY:	Yes, please.
	They both leave.
	Everything is quiet for a few moments.

Then the DEAD BODY, suddenly grabs the edges of the table he is lying on.

It's the CREATURE. He is tense. Maybe in pain. Maybe not. We can't know.

Slowly he turns his head to us.

He can see us. He looks at us for a few moments.

He doesn't blink.

4

VICTORIA:	How old were you?
MARY:	When I got married?
VICTORIA:	Yes.
MARY:	I just turned seventeen.
VICTORIA:	And did you love him?
MARY:	I was very fond of him.
	He got on with my father.
	They both liked horses. We didn't have any, but he did.
	He had lovely black hair. And strong hands.
	He also had nine brothers and sisters, I liked that very much.
VICTORIA:	Why?
MARY:	I don't know. Our house was always so desperately quiet.
VICTORIA:	How old was he?
MARY:	Let's see … He would have been twenty-one.
VICTORIA:	And what happened to him?
MARY:	He died. He went back home for a visit, just a few months after we got married.
	His mother was ill, and one of his sisters. Scarlet fever it turned out. All three of them dead within a week.
VICTORIA:	And then?

MARY:	I had to work. To support my parents.
	And your Mother needed help with the house.
VICTORIA:	Did you ever fall in love again?
MARY:	No.
VICTORIA:	How come?
MARY:	It just didn't happen.
VICTORIA:	Do you think it would have happened if you weren't looking after me. And then Elizabeth and William?
MARY:	It might have. It might have not.
VICTORIA:	Mary?
MARY:	Yes.
VICTORIA:	Do you ever think about the future?
MARY:	I do.
VICTORIA:	What do you think?
MARY:	I think about people who will come after us.
VICTORIA:	Do you think they will be different?
MARY:	In some ways. And in some ways not.
VICTORIA:	Do you think they will remember us?
MARY:	Of course.
VICTORIA:	How?
MARY:	They will read the books.
	Look at the paintings.
	They will be able to tell what we were like.
VICTORIA:	And do you think they will like us?
MARY:	That won't really matter.
VICTORIA:	How come?
MARY:	Well, we will be long dead, won't we.
VICTORIA:	Still. I think I would like them to like us.

MARY:	Why?
VICTORIA:	I don't know.
	It might mean we were right.

5

VICTORIA's house in Ingolstadt. Later that night.

The room is as it was when HENRY and VICTORIA left.

CREATURE is exactly where he was when they left.

At least one of them is drunk.

HENRY:	*(Off.)* After you.
VICTORIA:	*(Off.)* After you.
HENRY:	*(Off.)* No, after you.
VICTORIA:	*(Off.)* No, no, no, after you.

They both come in. VICTORIA is half a step ahead.

VICTORIA:	Well, thank you, Mr Clerval.
HENRY:	'Mr Clerval'.
	Makes it sound like as if you are talking to my father.
	'Mr Henry Clerval'.

HENRY gets a couple of glasses for the whiskey he brought in.

HENRY:	I can tell you right now, if I have a son, I won't call him Henry.
	–
	It's … selfish.
VICTORIA:	I think you would make an excellent father.
HENRY:	I wouldn't call him Henry.
VICTORIA:	I promise, you really don't have to.
	You can call him Lizzie?

HENRY laughs and pours them some whiskey.

HENRY: Victoria.

VICTORIA: Yes?

HENRY: What I am going to tell them? Your father, and Elizabeth.

About all this.

VICTORIA: I don't know, Henry.

What are you going to tell them?

HENRY drinks some of his whiskey.

HENRY: How do you know that what you are doing is not, you know, dangerous?

VICTORIA: Of course it is dangerous. It's science.

HENRY: I can't tell them that.

VICTORIA: We barely know anything.

There is this doctor, in England. Dr Snow. He believes that cholera is transmitted by water. Imagine that, Henry, the same water we drink, and cook with, and … make our whiskey with.

She takes a large sip of her whiskey.

VICTORIA: Just imagine if he is right, and cholera is not transmitted through pollution but through water supply – how many people have killed the ones they love, their own children, trying to wash off the bad air?

HENRY: And do you think he is right?

VICTORIA: I don't know. Dr Waldman says if all doctors just stopped practicing medicine for a year we would have a much healthier population.

HENRY: And do you like him, Dr Waldman?

VICTORIA: He's an alcoholic, but even drunk, he is head and shoulders above any other doctor at the University. Including me.

VICTORIA checks in on the RABBIT. He seems perfectly alive.

VICTORIA: *(Quietly to the RABBIT.)* Hello, hello there.

HENRY: So how does it feel, you know, having
                everything you ever wanted?

VICTORIA thinks about it for a moment.

VICTORIA: –

                It's pleasing.

HENRY: –

                I was hoping for a better answer.

VICTORIA: I know.

HENRY sits down.

VICTORIA: How is she?

HENRY: She wouldn't be able to be in this room, you
                know. With the animals and the chemicals
                and the …

VICTORIA: The dead body?

HENRY: Elizabeth is so kind. And patient.

VICTORIA: She's always loved you, you know that don't
                you?

HENRY: I do. I know. And I love her.

VICTORIA: So …

HENRY: But I don't know if I can be my father.

                What if I take over the business, and then ten
                year's down the line,

                I make her miserable because I'm bored with
                my life?

                –

                My father's house is dark. And it stinks.

                Yours is always bright.

                And people say exactly what they mean.

VICTORIA: Yes, they do.

HENRY: How come?

VICTORIA: You know, they have a wonderful linguistics department, right here at the University. You could both come.

HENRY: Impossible.

               She has to stay near your Father. Someone needs to look after him.

VICTORIA: That's not her job.

HENRY: No.

               It was yours.

VICTORIA takes the bottle off him.

VICTORIA: You are drunk.

HENRY: Yes. I am.

VICTORIA: Will you be staying the night?

HENRY: Not in this room. No.

VICTORIA: There is a spare room, upstairs.

HENRY: And if anyone sees me?

VICTORIA: Tell them you are my brother. It's barely a lie.

VICTORIA pours more whiskey into his glass, but keeps the bottle.

VICTORIA: Here.

HENRY: Victoria …

VICTORIA: Good night, Henry. We will talk tomorrow.

HENRY: –

               Right.

               Good night.

He leaves.

She is still for a few moments then smashes her glass against the wall.

She drinks from the bottle.

VICTORIA: My job.

She removes the curtain between her and the body.

She is used to be on her own with him. She is used to talking to him.

VICTORIA: What do you think?

Hm?

–

Do you think I should be at home, hm?

In a pretty dress.

Doing pretty … things.

She drinks some more.

VICTORIA: And what if I don't like pretty things?

Hm?

She turns away from him, still chatting away to him.

VICTORIA: What then?

CREATURE opens his eyes and looks at her for a moment. She can't see him yet.

VICTORIA: What happens then?

She turns back to him, and his eyes are closed again.

She notices that his head is not the way it was, it's turned a bit. She comes closer.

She lifts her hand to turn his head back when CREATURE's arms shoots up and he holds her forearm.

She freezes.

Slowly CREATURE opens his eyes, and looks at her.

They stare at each other for a few long moments.

She is showing him she means no harm.

Still holding her. CREATURE slowly sits up.

VICTORIA tries to step back. CREATURE, possibly accidentally, increases the grip and VICTORIA yelps. CREATURE is startled.

VICTORIA: It's … all right.

All right.

She is moving very slowly.

VICTORIA: Can you let me go?

CREATURE is listening.

VICTORIA: It's all right.

CREATURE: 'All. Right.'

CREATURE's voice is hoarse and it takes an effort to speak but the sound does come out.

VICTORIA: Oh.

VICTORIA doesn't try to move, she is letting CREATURE know she will not struggle.

Slowly, CREATURE lets go of her arm.

VICTORIA: Good.

Good.

She is observing it like a specimen, from all sides.

She touches his skin, he doesn't mind. She gently takes his wrist, to see if it bends.

CREATURE is observing her, alert and curious.

When she comes back to stand in front of him, he lifts his hand and touches her face.

She lets him.

VICTORIA: Hello.

CREATURE: 'Hello.'

VICTORIA laughs which makes CREATURE looks at her curiously.

VICTORIA: It's all right.

It's all going to be fine.

VICTORIA tilts her head to look at CREATURE's clavicle where she made a cut when infusing him with chemicals and draining blood.

As she tilts her head he tilts his. VICTORIA notices.

VICTORIA: Good. Good.

Can you do this?

She tilts her head the other way. CREATURE does as well.

VICTORIA: Excellent.

How about this?

She raises both of her arms in front of her.

VICTORIA: Can you?

CREATURE raises his arms and one can go all the way up but the other is too weak.

VICTORIA: All right.

She gently pushes his arms down.

VICTORIA: Can you look up?

She raises her hand above CREATURES head, expecting him to follow it just with his eyes. CREATURE moves the whole head, and looks up.

VICTORIA: All right. Never mind.

CREATURE now gently takes VICTORIA's arm and pulls it down, just as she did his. That amuses her.

VICTORIA: Good. Good.

–

Do you hurt?

CREATURE: 'Hurt'?

VICTORIA: Are you in pain?

CREATURE: –

She takes a needle and pricks her own finger.

VICTORIA: Ouch.

CREATURE is observing.

VICTORIA takes CREATURE's hand and gently pricks his finger with a needle.

VICTORIA: That? Can you feel that?

CREATURE is just looking at her. He doesn't feel it. Or at least not enough to care.

VICTORIA:　　　All right. And how about this?

She pinches the skin and slowly pushes the needle into CREATURES arm. CREATURE is still just looking at her, he doesn't comprehend what is expected of him, or what is going on.

She takes it out.

VICTORIA:　　　All right. Nothing.

She takes a scalpel from the table.

VICTORIA:　　　It's all right ... Give me your arm.

CREATURE just looks at her. VICTORIA gently takes his arm and cuts it beneath the elbow.

VICTORIA:　　　What about this?

No reaction from CREATURE.

VICTORIA:　　　Nothing? (Interesting.)

She turns his forearm and is about to make a larger cut along the forearm when CREATURE takes the scalpel from her hand and grabs her arm.

VICTORIA:　　　No.

She is measured and calm.

VICTORIA:　　　No... give that to me... There.

VICTORIA gently takes the scalpel from CREATURE's hand.

VICTORIA:　　　There.

VICTORIA gently guides CREATURE a step back, towards the table he was lying on.

VICTORIA:　　　Sit down. There.

VICTORIA leads CREATURE to lie down. She takes a large restraining belt and gives one side of it to CREATURE to hold.

VICTORIA:　　　Look. There we go.

CREATURE is lying down and holding one side of the belt. He doesn't understand what is going on. VICTORIA goes to the other side of the table and takes the other end of the restraining belt.

VICTORIA:　　　It's all right.

She takes both sides and secures them over CREATURE'S chest. She then secures two straps over his legs as well. CREATURE is strapped onto the bed.

CREATURE is not in pain and is patiently observing what she is doing.

VICTORIA: All right?

CREATURE: All. Right.

VICTORIA takes a scalpel from the side and stands over CREATURE. Her hands are above his chest.

VICTORIA: Don't worry. It will all be fine.

VICTORIA starts to cut down CREATURE'S chest and CREATURE screams in pain. He stands up tearing all the restraints in the process.

VICTORIA: No!

CREATURE stands up. He is stronger than she is.

VICTORIA: Sit down. Sit. Down!

CREATURE doesn't.

VICTORIA grabs the ether and a cloth from the bench. CREATURE is slowly coming towards her.

VICTORIA: No.

CREATURE has stopped a step away from her.

VICTORIA: That's right. It won't hurt.

VICTORIA slowly comes closer to him. Step by step. CREATURE is alert.

When she is close enough to him, VICTORIA tries to press the cloth into his face but CREATURE pulls her in and holds her tight.

VICTORIA: Let me go.

CREATURE: 'No'.

VICTORIA: Let. Me. Go.

CREATURE: 'No!'

VICTORIA puts all her weight into trying to get away but CREATURE puts all his weight against her and holds her down until she loses her consciousness.

CREATURE slowly stands up.

VICTORIA is on the ground. Still breathing but unconscious.

CREATURE looks at her.

CREATURE looks at us.

6

MARY sings a lullaby to VICTORIA.

7

ENGLAND. VICTORIA is asleep on her own bed.

There's lighting and thunder. VICTORIA wakes up.

She is not sure what happened. She looks around. She is home.

She goes to the window. She looks outside. There is just darkness.

She can hear voices coming from outside.

VICTORIA goes to leave but the doors are locked.

She tries again but she can't open them. She bangs on the door.

VICTORIA: Elizabeth …

              –

              Elizabeth.

There is laughter coming from the other side of the door.

VICTORIA: Elizabeth!

              Can you hear me? Elizabeth!

She bangs on the door but there is no reply. She goes to the window and takes a quick look outside. The doors open and ELIZABETH comes in.

ELIZABETH: What on earth is going on?

VICTORIA:	Did you not hear me?
	I couldn't get out.
ELIZABETH:	You shouldn't be getting out of bed anyway. Don't you remember what we agreed?
VICTORIA:	I'm fine.
	I just need some air. I need to get out.

VICTORIA goes to the door and tries them again, but they are locked.

VICTORIA:	Did you do this?
ELIZABETH:	Do what?
VICTORIA:	The doors!
	Why are they locked?
ELIZABETH:	Of course they are not locked.
VICTORIA:	–
ELIZABETH:	You need to get back into bed. Come on.
VICTORIA:	No.

ELIZABETH sits on the bed, and is waiting for VICTORIA to join her.

ELIZABETH:	Tell me. What is going on?
VICTORIA:	There's someone outside.
ELIZABETH:	Where?
VICTORIA:	Out there.
ELIZABETH:	Come here.

VICTORIA joins her on the bed.

ELIZABETH:	There is no one outside. It's just a storm.
VICTORIA:	I saw his eyes. Looking at me.
	I woke up and ... and I couldn't get out.
ELIZABETH:	What can I do for you?
VICTORIA:	No. / I was ...
ELIZABETH:	Are you hungry?
VICTORIA:	No.

How long was I asleep?

ELIZABETH: You needed the sleep.

After everything that's happened.

VICTORIA: What's happened?

ELIZABETH: Oh, no. Victoria. Did you forget?

VICTORIA: What has happened?

FATHER and HENRY walk in mid-conversation.

FATHER: The only option now is to send her away. Probably somewhere warm. Maybe Italy.

HENRY: Couple of months in Venice, in the fresh air, would be most useful.

FATHER: We will just have to wait, with the announcement, and with the wedding.

HENRY: Yes. Yes, of course.

VICTORIA tries to stand up but ELIZABETH stops her.

VICTORIA: What is going on?

ELIZABETH: Victoria.

VICTORIA: Elizabeth! What is going on?

ELIZABETH: Do we really have to do this every night?

VICTORIA: Do what?

JUSTINE runs in.

JUSTINE: The letter has arrived!

ELIZABETH lifts the leather restraint off the bed and straps one of VICTORIA's wrists into it.

VICTORIA: Elizabeth!

JUSTINE gives the letter to ELIZABETH.

ELIZABETH: Let's see.

FATHER and HENRY are on the other side of the room. ELIZABETH joins them.

HENRY: Good news?

ELIZABETH:	Yes. Very good.
JUSTINE:	It's a letter from Victoria.
HENRY:	Oh good.
FATHER:	What does she say?
VICTORIA:	What?
ELIZABETH:	She writes about the house ... and the lake ... she is enjoying the sun, and being in the garden ... oh, she's been learning Italian.
HENRY:	Wonderful.
FATHER:	And, is she coming back?
ELIZABETH:	Let's see ... yes, there it is.
	No. She says she will stay in Italy.
FATHER:	Thank God.
VICTORIA:	I didn't write that!
HENRY:	After all, it will be easier. For everyone.

JUSTINE runs out.

VICTORIA:	Henry!
HENRY:	It was getting so difficult, with her being around. We didn't know how to explain it to the children.
ELIZABETH:	I am so sorry my love.
VICTORIA:	Henry! What on earth is going on?
FATHER:	Yes, we can all hope things will be a bit easier now.

JUSTINE runs in.

JUSTINE:	The letter has arrived!
ELIZABETH:	Oh. Excellent. Let's see.
FATHER:	Is it from Victoria?
ELIZABETH:	Yes it is.
HENRY:	Is she managing to leave the house?

ELIZABETH: So ... she says she is looking forward to the spring. And the smell of flowers. She can't go into the garden any more... but the cook brings her fresh flowers from time to time. Oh. How lovely.

FATHER: I knew she was going to be fine.

VICTORIA: Henry ...

ELIZABETH: The window in her room looks into the garden, so she is asking if we can arrange for someone to move her bed closer to the window, so she can see outside.

HENRY: I don't know about that.

JUSTINE runs out.

FATHER: She is probably safer away from the window.

ELIZABETH: It's for the best.

JUSTINE runs in.

VICTORIA: Stop it, Justine! Stop it!

JUSTINE: The letter has arrived!

ELIZABETH: Let's see.

HENRY: It doesn't look like it's from Victoria.

FATHER: No, it looks expensive.

JUSTINE: It looks official.

ELIZABETH: It is not from her.

JUSTINE: What does it say?

ELIZABETH: It's from the hospital.

JUSTINE: Is that where she works?

ELIZABETH: No. Where she died.

JUSTINE: Oh.

ELIZABETH: They are informing us that we can collect the body before five o'clock and if there are no family or relatives to collect the body, the city will arrange for it to be buried in common ground.

HENRY: Well, that doesn't sound too bad.

FATHER: At least she won't be alone.

JUSTINE: And she will be in Italy.

ELIZABETH: She always loved Italy.

HENRY: She was learning Italian.

FATHER: I knew it was all going to end well.

HENRY takes ELIZABETH's hand.

HENRY: Now it will all be fine.

ELIZABETH: Thank God.

JUSTINE opens the door wide for all of them.

FATHER: Now. Would anyone like a nice strong cup of tea?

ELIZABETH: Oh, let's have tea!

HENRY: Wonderful.

JUSTINE holds the door open and they all leave laughing.

VICTORIA is horrified, on the bed. Scared, shocked and confused.

They slam the door behind them. VICTORIA screams.

ELIZABETH runs into the room and runs to VICTORIA. She shakes her gently, and taps her face.

ELIZABETH: Victoria! Victoria … wake up!

VICTORIA wakes up. ELIZABETH is kneeling next to her bed.

ELIZABETH: There you go … there, just a bad dream. I'm right here. It's all right.

VICTORIA lifts her arms, there is nothing tying her to the bed. There are no leather straps.

VICTORIA: I had a … nightmare.

ELIZABETH: I know. You are running a fever.

VICTORIA: You were here, and Henry, and Father.

ELIZABETH: You are burning up.

VICTORIA: You were all just waiting for me to die.

ELIZABETH: Oh, you silly girl.

VICTORIA: I couldn't ... I didn't know what to do.

And there was this creature, with these horrible green eyes, just outside.

ELIZABETH: How horrible.

VICTORIA: Staring at me.

ELIZABETH: I'll get a cold towel.

That should help for now.

VICTORIA: How long was I asleep?

ELIZABETH: You've been in and out for a couple of days.

VICTORIA: How ... how did I get here?

ELIZABETH: Henry brought you back from Ingolstadt.

You were ... you had a fever. You weren't really yourself.

VICTORIA: Was there anyone else?

ELIZABETH: Where?

VICTORIA: With us.

ELIZABETH: Of course not, who else would be there?

VICTORIA: Are you sure?

ELIZABETH: Father will be glad to hear you are finally awake.

VICTORIA: Is he here?

ELIZABETH: Of course. He is upstairs, asleep.

VICTORIA: And William?

ELIZABETH: He is in his room. And Justine and Mary, as well.

Everyone is just fine. I'll get you a towel.

VICTORIA: Don't leave me in here.

ELIZABETH:	I won't be a minute.
VICTORIA:	Please.
ELIZABETH:	–
VICTORIA:	Please.
ELIZABETH:	All right.
	Shall we get some hot milk? The way Mother used to make it.
VICTORIA:	Yes. I'd like that.
ELIZABETH:	(All right.) I think I heard Justine. Let's see if she will join us.

ELIZABETH helps VICTORIA out of bed, and they both go downstairs.

For a few moments it's all quiet.

Then there is lighting, and we see CREATURE, somewhere in the world, waiting for her, possibly in pain.

ACT II

8

CREATURE: Do you think I don't see you?

Do you?

You can't hide in the dark.

9

England. Frankenstein family House. Evening.

Drawing room. MARY and VICTORIA come in mid-conversation.

MARY: *(Off.)* It's no trouble at all...

VICTORIA: *(Off.)* Mary. I'll take them up in a minute.

MARY: Of course.

VICTORIA: Where is everyone?

MARY: Your father is in his study, and Elizabeth and Henry should be back any minute.

VICTORIA: Justine?

MARY: She is out with William.

VICTORIA takes it all in.

VICTORIA: –

It's very quiet.

MARY lingers at the door.

MARY: I'm glad you are back.

VICTORIA: Thank you, Mary.

MARY: Would you like me to make a pot of coffee?

VICTORIA: More than anything. Thank you.

ELIZABETH comes in. She wasn't expecting to see VICTORIA.

VICTORIA:　　　Hello.

ELIZABETH rushes to her and holds her tightly.

ELIZABETH:　　Oh, thank God. Thank God you are home.

VICTORIA:　　　It's good to be back.

ELIZABETH steps back and looks at VICTORIA.

ELIZABETH:　　You look older.

VICTORIA:　　　It's been barely a year.

ELIZABETH:　　Well, it suits you.

VICTORIA:　　　As kind as ever.

ELIZABETH:　　Have you talked to Father?

VICTORIA:　　　He's upstairs.

ELIZABETH:　　We should tell him you are back.

VICTORIA:　　　He knows.

ELIZABETH:　　Oh.

ELIZABETH takes off her coat.

VICTORIA:　　　Not much has changed.

ELIZABETH:　　You know us, we don't lead terribly exciting
　　　　　　　　lives.

VICTORIA:　　　How's Henry?

ELIZABETH:　　Busy. His father retired.

ELIZABETH shows VICTORIA the engagement ring.

VICTORIA:　　　When is the wedding?

ELIZABETH:　　As soon as we can get everyone in one place.

VICTORIA:　　　Congratulations.

ELIZABETH:　　He'll be surprised to see you.

VICTORIA observes ELIZABETH.

VICTORIA:　　　You look happy.

ELIZABETH: I am.

VICTORIA: Good.

ELIZABETH picks up something WILLIAM left lying around.

ELIZABETH: I swear I spend half of my day picking up
               after William.

MARY brings in the coffee.

VICTORIA: How is he? *(to MARY.)* Thank you, Mary.

ELIZABETH: Stubborn and lively. Won't be trapped inside
               if he can help it.

*ELIZABETH continues tidying the room. Mostly WILLIAM'S stuff
laying around.*

ELIZABETH: I thought you might write, might tell us
               where you are.

VICTORIA: I didn't know where I would be one week to
               another.

ELIZABETH: You didn't go back to Ingolstadt.

VICTORIA: No. I went to France. Then Switzerland.
               Holland. Then to London. Last few months I
               spent up north, in Scotland.

ELIZABETH: That's quite a journey.

VICTORIA: Yes, it is.

VICTORIA pours them both coffee.

ELIZABETH: So ... did you want to be in all those places,
               or did you just not want to be here?

VICTORIA: –

ELIZABETH: I might not be educated, but I'm not stupid,
               you know.

VICTORIA: I never thought that.

HENRY comes in.

HENRY: Whose trunk / is that at the ...

HENRY sees VICTORIA.

HENRY:	My God.
ELIZABETH:	Look who I found.

HENRY and VICTORIA hug. He's been worried about her as well.

HENRY:	How long are you staying?
ELIZABETH:	Oh, give her a second, Henry, she's just arrived.
VICTORIA:	Couple of weeks. *(To ELIZABETH.)* If that is all right?
ELIZABETH:	Of course it is. It's your home, you don't have to ask.

ELIZABETH takes a sip out of her cup, but then leaves it when she realises it's not tea.

HENRY:	So?
VICTORIA:	So?
HENRY:	Where have you been?
ELIZABETH:	It turns out, all over the world.
VICTORIA:	Just Europe.
HENRY:	And, how was it? How is Europe?
VICTORIA:	Quite angry.
HENRY:	Who with?
VICTORIA:	Mostly with itself these days.

VICTORIA pours HENRY some coffee as well.

HENRY:	Your Father will be happy to see you.
VICTORIA:	Yes. That's what everyone keeps telling me.
HENRY:	He missed you, you know.
VICTORIA:	How can you tell?
ELIZABETH:	Victoria.
HENRY:	He's been worried about you.
VICTORIA:	He is always worrying about something.
HENRY:	We all were.

ELIZABETH: More coffee?

VICTORIA: No, thank you.

ELIZABETH pours her some more anyway.

HENRY: What were you thinking just leaving like that?

VICTORIA: What was I thinking?

HENRY: Yes.

VICTORIA: I was thinking I am a grown woman and I don't have to justify my behaviour to anyone.

HENRY: And you couldn't wait for things to settle down?

VICTORIA: Why? There was no need.

HENRY: For weeks, you were barely conscious, and then as soon as you could walk, you run away.

VICTORIA: I didn't 'run away'.

HENRY: Do you know she didn't leave your room for a week?

ELIZABETH: Henry.

HENRY: Day and night sitting at your bed. You didn't know what was going on. You were hysterical.

VICTORIA: I most certainly wasn't 'hysterical'.

HENRY: Didn't you tell us someone is trying to kill you?

VICTORIA: You were there when I collapsed. You saw how exhausted I was. I hadn't slept for days.

ELIZABETH: Henry, she just got back. Can we / please leave it for now?

HENRY: / And that is it?

VICTORIA: Yes.

HENRY:	So no one is following you?
VICTORIA:	No.
HENRY:	And there is no one trying to kill you?
VICTORIA:	*(To ELIZABETH.)* Does that sounds plausible to you?
ELIZABETH:	Actually no, not at all.
VICTORIA:	I was just tired. That's all.

FATHER appears at the door.

FATHER:	I thought I heard voices.
VICTORIA:	Hello.
FATHER:	Victoria.
VICTORIA:	I just arrived.
FATHER:	Good. Good.
	Henry.
HENRY:	Dr Frankenstein.

FATHER doesn't come any further in.

VICTORIA:	You are looking well, Father.
FATHER:	I left my glasses somewhere around here.

FATHER looks for them.

FATHER:	Oh, there they are.

He gets them.

FATHER:	You see, I can't read without them anymore. Yes.
VICTORIA:	How is work?
FATHER:	These days I seem to spend more time at my desk than visiting patients.
VICTORIA:	That must be a good sign.
FATHER:	Yes. It must be. It must be.

They stand there for a moment, neither having much to say.

FATHER:	All right then.

FATHER is about to leave.

VICTORIA: I brought you something.

FATHER: You didn't have to.

VICTORIA gets a small parcel from her coat.

VICTORIA: I know. Here.

She hands it to him.

FATHER: What is it?

VICTORIA: They are called 'matches'.

FATHER: And what are they for?

VICTORIA: Here. Let me show you.

                   (To HENRY.) Can you help me?

HENRY: –

VICTORIA: Please?

HENRY helps VICTORIA take one of the oil lamps down. She blows out the flame.

ELIZABETH: Now why did you do that?

VICTORIA: Come here.

ELIZABETH does. HENRY doesn't.

VICTORIA: You press it against this bit here ... and ...

She strikes it.

VICTORIA: ... there you go.

The match burns for a few seconds in her hand and then she lights the lamp.

VICTORIA: Just like that.

ELIZABETH: Can you do it again?

VICTORIA: Why don't you have a go?

FATHER: Maybe you should leave it for now.

ELIZABETH: Let me try.

VICTORIA blows out the lamp, and shows ELIZABETH how to do it.

VICTORIA: Just press firmly. There …

ELIZABETH strikes it and the flame makes her laugh.

ELIZABETH: Look.

She brings it to the lamp and lights it.

FATHER is looking closely at the lamp. He is not too impressed with what he sees.

FATHER: It's not burning any different than it was five minutes ago.

VICTORIA: It makes things easier.

FATHER: Give them to Mary. She might find some use for them.

VICTORIA: –

              Of course.

FATHER: I asked her to prepare your old room for you.

VICTORIA: That won't be necessary.

FATHER: Why is that?

VICTORIA: I can't stay for long.

FATHER: Why not?

VICTORIA: I / need to …

ELIZABETH: / They are expecting her back in Ingolstadt.

VICTORIA looks at ELIZABETH.

ELIZABETH: They heard about her work since she left the university. And they would very much like her to continue the research back at her department, as soon as possible.

FATHER: I see.

              –

              I see.

              Well, Justine will be happy to have you back. Even for a short while.

She misses talking to you.

VICTORIA: And I miss her.

FATHER: Yes. You should tell her that sometimes.

Loud voices are heard from outside. MARY's scream.

For a moment no other sound comes from outside.

ELIZABETH: What was that?

Then the doors open wide and JUSTINE appears. She is wet and dirty with mud. She doesn't even register VICTORIA is back.

FATHER: What happened?

JUSTINE is looking at them all. One by one.

MARY appears behind her as well.

JUSTINE can't find the words.

FATHER: What happened?

JUSTINE: I am sorry. I am so so sorry.

JUSTINE just stands there staring at them all.

FATHER: Where is William?

JUSTINE can't say it.

FATHER: Where is William?

MARY: William is dead.

VICTORIA looks at HENRY who is staring at her.

MARY: He is dead, sir.

10

CREATURE: It is very, very different. When a child looks at you.

When he looks straight into your eyes.

There is no pity. No hatred. No challenge. No disgust.

Just –

–

Not like the others.

They are just there, judging only what they see.

Ready to change their mind at any time.

Ready to shout. To be bored. To run away. To smile.

Each of those things equally possible. Equally right.

Not like the others.

What do you think when you look at me?

Right now?

Who am I?

A monster. A beast. An animal.

Do you think I look like I stink?

Do you think I sound like I hate?

Is that it?

Am I right?

If it was just you and me on the street.

If it was cold. And dark.

You and me.

Would you invite me into your house?

Into your home?

May I sit at your table?

May I sleep in your bed?

(Please.)

Would you ask me who I am?

Or would you look away?

She never did.

Just like a child. Looking straight into my eyes.

Ready for anything.

She would be close, always so close. I could feel the warmth.

Warmth of her breath.

Just her and I.

Her voice always there. Dipping in and out.

Her sentences broken, sometimes slow, sometimes fast.

But always there, getting through to me, when there was nothing else.

Just darkness, and cold, and not knowing where, or who, or why.

When there was nothing, she was still there. Talking, always talking (to me).

Not like the others.

11

JUSTINE is in a cell. Some straw for a bed. Nothing else. VICTORIA and ELIZABETH are there.

ELIZABETH: Justine.

JUSTINE doesn't respond.

ELIZABETH: Justine.

JUSTINE: I told you, I am not going to lie.

ELIZABETH: It's not a lie.

JUSTINE: What is it then?

ELIZABETH: Just tell the judges what you saw. That's all. A man followed you. He attacked William. And he killed him.

JUSTINE:	It wasn't a man.
ELIZABETH:	(Oh.) For God's sake.
JUSTINE:	It wasn't.
ELIZABETH:	You were tired. And cold. And scared.
JUSTINE:	Victoria?
ELIZABETH:	She wasn't there.
VICTORIA:	You should do as Elizabeth says.
ELIZABETH:	You just need to describe him to the judges. You need to tell them what you remember.
JUSTINE:	It wasn't a man, Elizabeth, / it was a …
ELIZABETH:	Will you stop / saying it.
JUSTINE:	/ It was the / devil.
ELIZABETH:	There is no devil!

JUSTINE knows she is right, she knows what she saw.

JUSTINE:	That's what the judge said. That it can't be the devil.
	He said I'm lying about seeing it. He said for that I will go to hell. Where I will burn for ever.
ELIZABETH:	You won't.
JUSTINE:	You heard him say it.
ELIZABETH:	He didn't mean it.
JUSTINE:	Then why did he say it?
ELIZABETH:	He was just trying to find out what happened.
JUSTINE:	Is he saying there is no devil?. But there is hell? How can that be?
ELIZABETH:	He's agreed to hear you again. As a favour to the family. To me.
JUSTINE:	Elizabeth, how can there be one and not the other?

ELIZABETH: Justine, listen to me. It wasn't easy for me to ask.

JUSTINE: I've been sitting here all night, thinking about it. And I don't understand it.

               I know what I saw, and I don't want to lie, Elizabeth. I don't want to go to hell.

ELIZABETH: You are not listening to me.

JUSTINE: Are you listening to me?

JUSTINE is finding hard to accept this. She turns to VICTORIA for help.

JUSTINE: It wasn't a man. I know it wasn't a man.

VICTORIA: How do you know?

JUSTINE: I could see his eyes. There was no life in them.

VICTORIA: Did he say anything?

JUSTINE: No. He just stood there. Over William.

               Looking at me. With those horrible eyes.

               And then he did it.

VICTORIA: What did he do?

JUSTINE: He pounced on him, like an animal. He had his paws all over William's body.

               I thought he was going to break him in half.

ELIZABETH: We don't need to hear any more.

JUSTINE: That is the truth.

ELIZABETH: Do you understand what is going to happen to you if the judges decide you are guilty?

JUSTINE: Yes.

ELIZABETH: Do you?

JUSTINE: I do.

ELIZABETH: Tell me.

JUSTINE: I am going to die.

ELIZABETH:	How?
VICTORIA:	Elizabeth / there is no need ...
ELIZABETH:	You be quiet now. How, Justine? How are you going to die?
JUSTINE:	They are going to execute me.
ELIZABETH:	How?
JUSTINE:	They are going to hang me.
ELIZABETH:	Yes, they will. And do you think it will hurt?
JUSTINE:	I don't know / if it will ...
ELIZABETH:	Of course you do. Think about it.
	Do you think it will hurt? Being hung off a piece of wood, like an animal, with the thick rope around your neck. What do you think – is that going to hurt?
JUSTINE:	Yes.
ELIZABETH:	And how long do you think it would take?
JUSTINE:	I don't know.
ELIZABETH:	How long do you think it would take?
JUSTINE:	A while?
ELIZABETH:	It will take forever.
JUSTINE:	I don't / want to ...
ELIZABETH:	And while you are hanging, struggling to breathe, to see, to hear, while you are trashing for your life, you will lose control over your bowls, in front of everyone, and if it's still taking too long, they will send someone to pull on your legs and finish it for you.
JUSTINE:	–
ELIZABETH:	Is that really how you want to die?
JUSTINE:	No.

ELIZABETH: Good.

               So.

               Will you tell the judges you saw a man kill William, and not a devil?

JUSTINE: –

ELIZABETH: Justine?

JUSTINE: I don't think I can. It would be a lie.

               And I'm scared to lie.

ELIZABETH can't believe anyone can think this way.

VICTORIA knows a bit more about what it means to know you are right, even if the whole world thinks differently.

ELIZABETH: I tried.

JUSTINE: Please, don't be angry / with me ...

ELIZABETH: So ungrateful.

JUSTINE: Don't / say that ...

ELIZABETH: I will pray for you, Justine.

JUSTINE: Please ...

ELIZABETH: We all will. I am sorry.

ELIZABETH leaves.

JUSTINE: Elizabeth!

But ELIZABETH is gone. VICTORIA is quiet.

For a few moments there is nothing to be said.

JUSTINE: She must hate me.

VICTORIA: No, she doesn't. She is just scared. And she loves you very much.

VICTORIA sits next to JUSTINE. They are comfortable in each other's company.

JUSTINE: Do you think ...

VICTORIA: What?

JUSTINE: Do you think, I might be wrong?

VICTORIA:	How? .
JUSTINE:	I don't know.
	Maybe there's something wrong with my mind. Or with my eyes?
VICTORIA:	Do you think there is?
JUSTINE:	No. Do you?
VICTORIA:	No. I don't.
JUSTINE:	So you believe me?

VICTORIA thinks she knows what happened.

JUSTINE:	Do you?
VICTORIA:	How close were you?
JUSTINE:	This close.
VICTORIA:	Could see if he had any kind of mark on him?
JUSTINE:	Like what?
VICTORIA:	A scar. Here. And here.
JUSTINE:	–
VICTORIA:	Did you see anything like that?
JUSTINE:	How do you know?
VICTORIA:	There's nothing wrong with your mind, or your eyes.
JUSTINE:	Did you see him too? Did you?
VICTORIA:	Yes. I did.
JUSTINE:	So he's not a devil?
VICTORIA:	No...
JUSTINE:	*(JUSTINE crosses herself.)* Thank God.
VICTORIA:	... but he's not a man either.
JUSTINE:	What is he then?
VICTORIA:	I don't know.

JUSTINE:	Was it him you saw when … when you got ill?
VICTORIA:	Yes.
JUSTINE:	Was it him who made you ill?
VICTORIA:	No. Yes. I don't know. Maybe.
	I think I hurt him.
JUSTINE:	Is that why he killed William?
VICTORIA:	I don't know that either.

JUSTINE is trying to hold all this information in her head.

JUSTINE:	Will you tell the judges?
VICTORIA:	Tell them what?
JUSTINE:	What you told me.
VICTORIA:	I can't.
JUSTINE:	Why not?
VICTORIA:	They wouldn't believe me.
JUSTINE:	Of course they would. You are – you.
VICTORIA:	They won't, Justine.
JUSTINE:	But I believe you.
VICTORIA:	You are smarter than they are.
JUSTINE:	So … what do I do now?
VICTORIA:	You should tell them you saw a man, a person. It's not a lie.
JUSTINE:	People are alive. And this thing, he isn't, is he?
VICTORIA:	No.
JUSTINE:	Than that would be a lie. I can't do that.
VICTORIA:	What would you like to do?
JUSTINE:	I would like to tell the truth. And let God decide.
VICTORIA:	Then that's what you do. You tell the truth.

JUSTINE is at peace.

JUSTINE: Thank you.

                  Thank you.

12

CREATURE: *(Shows us a scar.)* This one was first: One
                  man. A knife. Trying to defend himself. I
                  wasn't going to hurt him. My legs didn't
                  work, I was trying to stand up.

                  This was the second: A guard. In the asylum.
                  A stick. Maybe a pipe. For not answering
                  his question. My head was still muddy. The
                  words so pale. Still in the distance. I couldn't
                  reach them. All I could do was make a
                  sound.

                  This one: I don't know who. Middle of the
                  night. I don't know why.

                  This one: Two guards. Same knife. One, then
                  the other, one, then the other. The rest in the
                  circle, watching, cheering. Waiting to see if
                  they can draw blood.

                  I don't bleed.

                  This one: A woman. Out on the street.
                  Scared of seeing me in the dark. Protecting
                  herself. Terrified.

                  Terrified. Of me.

                  (Another scar.) Fight. *(Another scar.)* Frost.
                  (Another scar.) A speeding carriage.

*There is a big scar right across his chest, the one he didn't mention,
the one she made. The first one. He skips that one.*

                  (Another scar.) This one is: me. *(Another scar.)*
                  And this one: a dog I tried to touch.

13

England. Family house. Dining room. HENRY and VICTORIA.

VICTORIA: Do you think she wanted us to be there?

HENRY: No. She wouldn't want you to see her die.

HENRY checks the time.

VICTORIA: She asked for a Sunday dress.

HENRY: –

VICTORIA: You wouldn't think that would make a difference, would you?

VICTORIA pours herself a drink.

HENRY: Victoria?

VICTORIA: Yes.

HENRY: What really happened to William?

VICTORIA: How would I know?

HENRY: Does it have anything to do with what you were doing in Ingolstadt?

VICTORIA: What do you mean?

HENRY: You showed me something that day.

VICTORIA: My work. Yes.

HENRY: The body. And the rabbit.

VICTORIA: What about it? I had dozens of them.

HENRY: But when I found you …

VICTORIA: Yes?

HENRY: It wasn't there, was it? That thing.

You know what I'm talking about. The man. The body.

VICTORIA: Henry.

HENRY: Yes?

VICTORIA: You need to stop asking me about this.

HENRY:	Why?
VICTORIA:	You don't want to know.
HENRY:	What if I do?
VICTORIA:	Do you?
HENRY:	Yes. I do.
VICTORIA:	Are you certain?
HENRY:	Yes.
VICTORIA:	All right.
	Ask me.
	Ask me.
HENRY:	What happened to William?
VICTORIA:	He was killed by the man you saw when you came to visit.
HENRY:	One that was dead?
VICTORIA:	Yes.
HENRY:	And is now … alive?
VICTORIA:	Yes.
HENRY:	Why?
VICTORIA:	I don't know.
HENRY:	Did you know he was going to do it?
VICTORIA:	Of course not. I thought he was gone.
HENRY:	And Justine …
VICTORIA:	Yes?
HENRY:	She was telling the truth? When she said it was a daemon.
VICTORIA:	Yes. That was the only way her mind could explain what she saw.
HENRY:	So she is innocent?
VICTORIA:	Yes.
HENRY:	And she is about to die?

VICTORIA: Yes.

HENRY: Why didn't you say something?

VICTORIA: No one would believe me if I told them the truth.

HENRY: How do you know?

VICTORIA: Think about it. Would you? If you haven't seen it yourself.

HENRY: You could have tried.

VICTORIA: No. That would be the end of my work. I would lose everything I've achieved so far.

HENRY: It's not always about you, you know.

VICTORIA: It's never about me, Henry. It's about what I can do.

HENRY: –

VICTORIA: Just think about it, if I am right, if I can find a way to stop people dying – from filthy water, from a cough, from a mosquito bite, from childbirth – if I can do that, if I can stop all that suffering ... is it not my duty to try?

HENRY: –

VICTORIA: You remember how much it hurts, don't you? What it does to you when someone you love suddenly disappears. When they die

    What if I could stop all that pain? For everyone. For ever.

    Wouldn't that be a good thing?

HENRY: So you will let Justine die.

VICTORIA: It's one for the sake of millions.

HENRY: You are playing God.

VICTORIA: I would be if God was the one that created life.

    But he didn't. I did.

HENRY: And look at how that ended?

VICTORIA: We are not at the end, we are at the very start.

FATHER is at the door.

FATHER: When your Mother was alive, there was no shouting in this house.

VICTORIA: I didn't see you.

FATHER: She knew how to ... how to do all this.

HENRY: If there is / anything I can do...

FATHER: / She used to say there is a lesson in everything.

What do you think, Henry, what is our lesson in all this?

HENRY: I'm afraid I don't know.

FATHER: No. I don't know either.

HENRY: We were just waiting for Elizabeth.

FATHER: She will stay in her room. She wants to be praying when it happens.

FATHER checks his pocket watch.

FATHER: It's almost time.

FATHER sits down. So does HENRY.

FATHER: Sit down.

She does. They all sit in silence for a while longer.

FATHER takes out his watch, keeps it out for a bit then puts it back into his pocket.

FATHER: *(FATHER crosses himself.)* God bless her soul.

HENRY: *(So does HENRY.)* God bless her.

VICTORIA takes a sip of her drink.

FATHER: Henry, would you mind giving me a moment with my daughter?

HENRY: Of course. I will check on Elizabeth.

He stops for a moment before leaving.

HENRY: Victoria.

VICTORIA: Henry.

HENRY leaves. The two of them have never said goodbye like this.

FATHER: Sit down.

VICTORIA: I'm fine, thank you.

FATHER: It's all right, you know, if you want to…

VICTORIA: What?

FATHER: If you want to cry.

VICTORIA: Thank you.

She doesn't. FATHER goes to the drinks table.

FATHER: You've grown up these last few years.

VICTORIA: Does that come as a surprise?

FATHER: You might not believe it, but it always does.

FATHER pours himself a drink.

FATHER: You will need to be kinder to Elizabeth.

                Especially now Justine is gone.

VICTORIA: –

FATHER: You will also need to think about coming back. Someone will need to look after the house.

VICTORIA: I can't.

FATHER: Of course you can.

VICTORIA: I am not going to leave my work. It's too important.

FATHER: Is that so?

VICTORIA: –

                Yes.

FATHER: I see. And do you think the work you do at the University is more important than what I do here?

VICTORIA: I know it is.

FATHER: Tell me, what is more important than being there for another human being? Helping them when they are ill? When they need you the most?

VICTORIA: Helping thousands. Maybe millions.

FATHER: Oh for Gods sake, is that what you think you are doing?

VICTORIA: Father?

FATHER: Yes.

VICTORIA: Why are you always so angry with me?

MARY opens the door.

MARY: Excuse me.

FATHER: What is it, Mary?

MARY: There is a man downstairs. He is asking to see Dr Frankenstein.

FATHER: A patient?

MARY: I don't think so.

FATHER: Then tell him I'm busy. He can come later.

MARY: –

I believe he is here to see Dr Victoria Frankenstein.

VICTORIA: Did he tell you his name?

MARY: No. It's a foreign gentleman.

He says you will know him from Germany.

VICTORIA: Let him in, Mary.

MARY: Would you like me to put on a pot of tea?

VICTORIA: Coffee, please. Thank you.

MARY: Of course.

MARY leaves.

FATHER: Your mother never drank tea either.

FATHER leaves his drink on the table.

FATHER: I told her, you know. I told her I wouldn't know how to do this without her. I was the most unfit person for this office and she was the best qualified in the world.

 And then she left us anyway.

VICTORIA: I really wish that wasn't true.

FATHER: I know.

 I know.

FATHER pick up his glasses and leaves.

VICTORIA finishes her drink. She turns around and the CREATURE is standing in the room.

For a few moments they just stare at each other. Neither moves.

CREATURE takes in the room.

He comes closer to VICTORIA.

They observe each other.

VICTORIA speaks first.

VICTORIA: There are others in the house.

CREATURE: –

VICTORIA: They will hear me if I shout.

CREATURE: Do they know about me?

VICTORIA: No.

CREATURE: Why?

VICTORIA: I didn't think you would survive.

CREATURE: I did.

VICTORIA: Yes. You did.

 How?

CREATURE sees she is looking at him differently than before.

CREATURE: Do you hate me?

VICTORIA: No.

                I don't feel anything for you.

CREATURE comes close to her and VICTORIA freezes.

He leans in and smells her. He gently touches her. He can feel her warmth.

She moves her head away from his stench.

CREATURE: Look at me.

She doesn't.

CREATURE: Look at me!

She does.

CREATURE: What do you see?

He comes closer.

CREATURE: What do you see?

VICTORIA: –

                A monster.

CREATURE: I heard that word before.

                A 'monster'.

VICTORIA: You killed a child.

CREATURE: –

                You are not kind to me.

VICTORIA: Why would I be?

CREATURE: You used to be.

                You used to tell me everything.

VICTORIA: –

CREATURE: Didn't you?

VICTORIA: I didn't know you were there.

CREATURE: And yet I was. Like a slab of meat.

VICTORIA: I thought you were dead.

CREATURE: And then you didn't. You saw me stand up.

              You helped me walk.

              Do you remember?

              Do you?

VICTORIA: I do.

CREATURE: You were happy.

              You laughed with me.

              You sat with me.

              You touched me.

              And then you cut me.

              Didn't you?

VICTORIA: –

CREATURE: Didn't you?

VICTORIA: Yes, I did.

CREATURE: Why?

VICTORIA: It is my job.

*CREATURE looks at the room again. It's not telling him much
about her.*

CREATURE: Did you ever wonder what happened to me?

VICTORIA: No.

CREATURE: –

VICTORIA: Yes.

CREATURE: Just grabbed off the street, taken away. Like
              an animal. You see, I tried to explain, I tried
              to tell them about you, but I had no voice.
              Nothing.

              I had all the words, up here, but they
              wouldn't come out.

VICTORIA: –

CREATURE: Have you ever heard an animal when it's
               being slaughtered?

               Have you?

VICTORIA: Yes.

CREATURE: That's what men sound like when you take
               away the part that is human, when you lock
               them up.

VICTORIA: I didn't know.

CREATURE: You do now.

VICTORIA: –

CREATURE: –

VICTORIA: What happened?

CREATURE: This?

VICTORIA: Yes.

CREATURE: The guards.

This is not enough for VICTORIA to understand what he means.

CREATURE: They were amused that I don't bleed. A
               game. Almost a competition.

VICTORIA: Did it hurt?

CREATURE: I don't know.

               Maybe.

               The world was still wrong way round. I
               could touch the smells, see the words, and
               smell colour.

               The pain, I could hear – so I didn't know if it
               was mine, or everyone else's.

VICTORIA: Does it hurt now?

CREATURE: –

               (Yes.) It does.

VICTORIA takes a step closer and looks at the scar. She moves slowly and carefully. She moves his collar and reveals a bit of scarred skin. He is letting her do this.

She touches the scar. CREATURE doesn't remember being touched without hate, it hasn't happened in a very long time. Just for a moment he relaxes into the touch.

She gently presses the scar. CREATURE grabs her hand. VICTORIA freezes. It's too similar to the first time they met.

CREATURE: No.

CREATURE brings her hand closer to his face and smells her skin.

CREATURE: I remember this. This smell.

When there was nothing. Just cold. And darkness.

Then this smell. And you.

VICTORIA: –

CREATURE: But nothing before that. Why?

What was before – this?

VICTORIA: I don't know.

CREATURE: Who. Does.

VICTORIA tries to take a step back, but he is still holding her arm.

CREATURE: There it is again. Fear. Anger. Frustration. Curiosity. Disgust.

He has read her correctly.

CREATURE: Do you know what's it like to be looked at like this by everyone?

Seeing them how they look at everyone else, and then how they look at you.

Do you?

VICTORIA: No.

CREATURE: What do you think I can I feel when all I get is – this.

Just anger and fear. And nothing else.

Not from a dog. Not from a child.

Not even from you.

He lets her go. He turns away from her and sees his own reflection in the mirror.

He goes closer. He looks into his own eyes.

CREATURE: You did this. Didn't you? This.

He knows who could look at him without hate.

CREATURE: Didn't you?

VICTORIA: Yes.

CREATURE: So you will make it better.

VICTORIA: How?

CREATURE: You will make another one.

Someone who can look at me and not feel – that.

VICTORIA: No.

CREATURE: Yes. You will.

Before you do anything for anyone else, you will do this.

VICTORIA: I don't know if I can.

CREATURE: You will try.

You will make me a family.

He finally takes his eyes off the mirror.

CREATURE: Or I will take yours.

ELIZABETH comes in. She is startled when she sees CREATURE, but quickly hides it.

ELIZABETH: I'm sorry.

CREATURE nods gently. She nods back. She is not sure why she did it.

ELIZABETH: I didn't know anyone was here.

CREATURE: Do we have an agreement?

He looks at ELIZABETH.

VICTORIA: We do.

CREATURE comes closer and offers his hand to VICTORIA. She shakes it.

He pauses next to ELIZABETH before he leaves.

CREATURE: *(To ELIZABETH.)* A pleasure.

CREATURE leaves.

ELIZABETH: What happened to him?

VICTORIA: Nothing.

ELIZABETH goes to the drinks table. While she speaks she opens a few bottles and smells them, until she finds the one she likes.

ELIZABETH: It's funny, I've been wanting to tell mother about it. About Justine. And William. I keep catching myself.

    I wonder what she would think of it all.

VICTORIA: She would probably know what to say. And what to do.

ELIZABETH has found a drink she wants but doesn't know which glass to use.

ELIZABETH: Which one?

VICTORIA: That one.

ELIZABETH pours herself a drink. She pours the same for VICTORIA.

VICTORIA: Elizabeth?

ELIZABETH: Yes?

VICTORIA: Would your life be easier if I didn't exist? If you were adopted by a family that didn't already have a child.

ELIZABETH thinks about it.

ELIZABETH: Probably. Yes.

VICTORIA: –

ELIZABETH: But an easy life doesn't make a good life.

VICTORIA: What does?

ELIZABETH: I wish I knew.

ELIZABETH has her first drink. MARY comes in.

ELIZABETH: *(Re drink.)* Yes. I see why you do this.

MARY: Dinner is ready whenever you are.

VICTORIA: Thank you, Mary.

MARY is about to leave.

ELIZABETH: Mary?

MARY: Yes.

ELIZABETH: –

                 Would you like to join us? Have a drink with
                 us?

MARY: –

ELIZABETH: –

MARY: Well ... that is very kind of you. But, no,
                 thank you.

ELIZABETH: All right. I'll ask Henry to build a fire later.
                 Just in case you change your mind.

MARY smiles. So does ELIZABETH.

MARY: I will be downstairs.

ELIZABETH: Thank you, Mary.

MARY leaves.

VICTORIA: What was that?

ELIZABETH: Did you never see them?

VICTORIA: Who?

ELIZABETH: I used to sneak out late at night and come
                 downstairs, when we were little. Mother
                 and Mary would be sitting in front of the
                 fireplace, each with a drink, talking and
                 laughing.

VICTORIA: And where was I?

ELIZABETH: Asleep.

VICTORIA: What did they talk about?

ELIZABETH: I don't know. Us. Books. People in town. Anything really.

VICTORIA: Do you think they knew you were there?

ELIZABETH: I think there is very little the two of them didn't know.

VICTORIA: I never knew.

ELIZABETH: I know.

–

Do you think – do you think they might be together?

VICTORIA: Who?

ELIZABETH: Mother and William. And Justine.

VICTORIA: –

ELIZABETH: I'd like to think they are.

VICTORIA: They can't / really be together because

ELIZABETH: / For God's sake. I let you believe what you want to believe, why can't you do the same for me?

Just for one moment.

Just once.

VICTORIA: I don't know.

I don't know.

ELIZABETH finishes her drink and puts down the glass.

ELIZABETH: You are not staying, are you?

VICTORIA: Yes.

ELIZABETH: Then it's best if you leave soon. This week if you can.

I think it would be easier for everyone.

VICTORIA:	And what about you? What about the wedding?
ELIZABETH:	That can wait a bit. Henry and I are not staying either.
VICTORIA:	Where are you going?
ELIZABETH:	London first, then India. He is selling the business (factory.). And we can start again. We thought it was the best.
VICTORIA:	That's sounds wonderful.
ELIZABETH:	It will be.

She hugs VICTORIA.

| ELIZABETH: | It will all be all right, you know.

Everything will be all right. |

ELIZABETH leaves.

14

| CREATURE: | I am not like you. We are different.
Our difference is great. It is profound.
I am dead.
You are alive.
I am dead.
You are alive.
That's a profound fucking difference, I'd say.
(But) It doesn't make you better.
It doesn't make you luckier.
It doesn't make you more powerful.
It just means you are going to die.
Sooner or later. Something, or someone, is going to kill you.
It might be an accident. Or retribution.
And you know I am right. |

–

The arrogance.

I can see you. 'The people'. On the street. In your homes.

Darting from one place you know to another.

On different streets. In different houses.

But all the same.

Taken individually, one by one, you are kind.

Some scared. Some in love.

Some angry and some just drunk.

But step back and look at you from a distance, and that is all you can see.

The arrogance.

'The people'.

You think your violence should not be met with violence. You are surprised when it is.

You think there is a virtue in where you are born, who you were born to or how you sound.

You see the injustice, and you lie to yourself about not being important or powerful enough or wealthy enough to stop it. You lie to yourself that your silence is not all it requires to continue.

Don't you?

You kill each other. Rape each other.

Enslave, torture, poison each other. And you fear – me? You huddle in your special little cave with your little family and fear the 'monster' in the dark.

–

Oh, the arrogance.

I am not like you. We are different.

And there will be another one like me.

We will go far away from you and find a
different way to be.

We will do nothing as you do it.

We will not lie.

We will not forget that we are already dead.

15

*Bavaria. House in Ingolstadt. It's messy from the last time VICTORIA
was there.*

Someone is unlocking the doors from outside. The doors open.

VICTORIA is standing at the door holding her trunk.

*She is reluctant to come in. Eventually she does. Room is empty. The only
light is coming from the outside. She doesn't close the door yet.*

*She gets a packet of matches from her pocket, finds a lamp and strikes
a match.*

ELIZABETH: You really shouldn't be doing that.

> *VICTORIA turns around to see her sister. ELIZABETH is sitting on
> the sofa.*

ELIZABETH: At least not in the dark.

VICTORIA: –

ELIZABETH: I am just saying.

VICTORIA: Well, I wouldn't have to do it if it wasn't
                dark.

ELIZABETH: And therein lies your problem.

> *VICTORIA lights the lamp and puts it back. She closes the doors.*
>
> *She gets another lamp.*

ELIZABETH: You are not going to light them all, are you?

VICTORIA: Of course I will.

ELIZABETH: Late at night, you see, that's usually when the
                fire starts.

VICTORIA: I know what I'm doing. I'm not going to start a fire.

ELIZABETH blows the flame out of the first lamp.

VICTORIA: Elizabeth!

ELIZABETH: This late, no one would hear us, if we were to shout.

VICTORIA has to light the lamp again.

ELIZABETH: And with the wind tonight, the whole neighbourhood would burn down.

VICTORIA: You are talking rubbish.

With the lights on VICTORIA takes her trunk inside. She looks around. It's messy.

No one has been in for a very long time.

ELIZABETH: When your Mother and I first met we would pretend we were married.

VICTORIA: What did you say?

FATHER appears. It's him talking and not ELIZABETH.

FATHER: We used to pretend we were married.

              We would sit at the table at her Father's house and pretend to talk about books and drink wine.

VICTORIA: What do you mean 'pretend'?

FATHER: We were fifteen. We didn't know anything about either.

VICTORIA: –

              Why are you telling me this?

FATHER: You asked me.

VICTORIA: No I didn't.

ELIZABETH: How can you live in such a mess? You really should have someone to help you.

VICTORIA takes few more things from the floor, and puts them away.

ELIZABETH: Mary could come and live with you.

VICTORIA: Will you give me a moment. I just arrived.

FATHER: She was so beautiful.

VICTORIA: Would you both, please, please shut up.

FATHER: Of course.

ELIZABETH: If that's what you want.

VICTORIA: –

               Thank you.

VICTORIA takes the sheets off the sofa where she used to sleep. She throws them on the ground. FATHER and ELIZABETH are patiently just sitting/ standing around. Waiting.

VICTORIA brings new linen from another room, and starts making the bed.

HENRY: Would you like some help?

HENRY appeared as well.

VICTORIA: I'm fine.

ELIZABETH: I don't think she wants us to talk to her?

HENRY: I just wanted to help in case she is forgetting something.

VICTORIA: I can make the bed on my own. Thank you.

HENRY: Why is she angry?

ELIZABETH: I think she is just tired.

FATHER: She's been traveling all night.

VICTORIA turns around and looks at three of them. She takes a deep breath in a hope they might go away. They don't.

FATHER: You should really get some sleep.

VICTORIA: I have work to do.

FATHER: You can't work at four in the morning.

VICTORIA: It wouldn't be the first time.

FATHER: But you might make a mistake, forget
               something.

VICTORIA: I won't.

FATHER: You can't say I didn't warn you.

VICTORIA hears a voice behind her.

JUSTINE: You won't forget me, will you?

VICTORIA turns to see JUSTINE.

They look at each other.

VICTORIA: No.

               Of course not.

JUSTINE: There was a crowd, you know.

               They all came to see me.

               I didn't cry.

               When they turned me off.

               It was very quick.

               My conscience was clear.

               I didn't lie.

               They let me hold the prayer book.

               I said a prayer for their souls.

               –

               And I asked them, for the sake of decency,
               not to hang me high.

VICTORIA: –

JUSTINE: You should be more careful, with the
               matches. You don't want to start a fire.

VICTORIA: Don't worry. I won't.

HENRY: Oh, can you smell that?

ELIZABETH: These will have to be washed all over again.

FATHER: Mary will do it. Or give it to Justine, she
               doesn't mind.

JUSTINE: I don't.

VICTORIA: Just leave it be. They are fine where they are.

VICTORIA goes to the washstand and finds some water in the container next to it. She takes her shirt off. She soaks a cloth and washes herself.

The apparitions are patiently waiting. She is ignoring the fact that they can see her half naked.

HENRY: Can I help you?

VICTORIA: God no!

HENRY: I just thought, in case you are forgetting something…

VICTORIA: –

HENRY: Forget I asked.

VICTORIA: I really wish I could.

And then she remembers what it was she forgot.

VICTORIA: No…

VICTORIA looks at HENRY.

HENRY: I'm sorry.

VICTORIA: No… no.

She rushes to the cage where Prometheus, the RABBIT, used to live. For a few moments she stands next to the cage.

She slowly opens the cage and looks in.

She looks at everyone else. They are not saying anything, they all feel for her.

VICTORIA: No.

She gently takes the dirty cloth he was on, and its body in it. She pulls him out, and holds him close.

VICTORIA: No.

She doesn't want to put him down.

She is holding him in her arms.

She sits on the bed holding the RABBIT wrapped in the cloth.

She can't touch it. She can't stop looking at it.

VICTORIA: I'm sorry.

She doesn't know what else to say.

VICTORIA: I am so so so sorry.

The apparitions kindly stand around her.

VICTORIA: I didn't mean to ...

As she curls up ...

FATHER gently helps her lie down.

HENRY lifts her legs onto the bed.

JUSTINE pulls the cover up and

ELIZABETH tucks her in.

VICTORIA: I am so sorry ...

Eventually they all slowly leave/disappear one by one. VICTORIA is left on her own, curled up in her bed with the RABBIT, quietly talking to him. Wrapped up in her grief.

On the other side of the room CREATURE turns around and looks at us. He's been there all the time, he's been waiting for her. He goes closer. He is moving with effort. He sits down. He will wait until the morning.

Several hours pass. Its dawn.

VICTORIA is asleep and CREATURE is sitting where he was. For a while he just sits there.

Quietly. Listening to her breathe. Then he speaks.

CREATURE: You breathing has changed.

              You are awake.

VICTORIA doesn't move.

CREATURE: It's all right. You can speak now.

Very slowly, VICTORIA sits up. For a few moments she is not sure if this is a dream.

It's not. She looks at the doors. They are closed.

CREATURE: There is no one else. Just you and I.

VICTORIA is fully awake now.

CREATURE: I was waiting for you.

VICTORIA: Were you here last night?

CREATURE: I was.

VICTORIA: –

CREATURE: You were sad.

VICTORIA: I was angry.

CREATURE: And sad.

CREATURE is looking at the RABBIT in VICTORIA's bed.

CREATURE: What is that?

VICTORIA: Nothing.

CREATURE: He is dead.

VICTORIA: Yes.

CREATURE goes to take it.

VICTORIA: Don't ... just leave it ...

CREATURE picks Prometheus up. He holds him.

CREATURE: Did you kill him?

VICTORIA: No.

              Yes.

              I don't know.

CREATURE: He is so small.

VICTORIA: –

CREATURE: So light.

VICTORIA: Could you please put him down?

CREATURE doesn't.

CREATURE: Was he yours?

VICTORIA: Yes.

CREATURE: Did you love him?

VICTORIA: –

He was just an animal.

CREATURE: Yes.

CREATURE gives Prometheus to her. She gently takes him.

CREATURE: Just an animal.

She takes Prometheus and takes him to the cage. She gently puts him in.

CREATURE: What happened to him?

VICTORIA: I left him alone. I left him alone for too long. So he died.

CREATURE: How did he die?

VICTORIA: He rotted. From inside. And I wasn't there to see it. Maybe stop it.

CREATURE: Was he like me? Was he an experiment?

VICTORIA: Yes. He was.

CREATURE: And is this going to happen to me?

VICTORIA: –

I hope so.

CREATURE is standing above Prometheus looking at his little body.

CREATURE: You were not going to help me, were you?

VICTORIA: No.

CREATURE: Why not?

VICTORIA: You are dangerous, you are a murderer. Why would I make another one?

CREATURE: How do you know?

VICTORIA: –

CREATURE: How do you know I'm dangerous?

VICTORIA: You attacked me.

CREATURE: After you cut me.

VICTORIA: You killed my brother.

CREATURE: No. I didn't.

VICTORIA: I know you killed William.

VICTORIA is staring at him. CREATURE stands up. He is moving with effort.

CREATURE: I didn't.

VICTORIA: –

CREATURE: I saw them leave. Him and the woman. They went to the river. I followed them. I thought … I thought he was so young, so happy, I thought maybe he can look at me and not hate me.

He was running around, close to the river, too close. One moment he was there, and the next he wasn't. He just slipped in, into the river. She didn't see it. She had her back to him. His head went under, and then his arm, and then he just disappeared.

I went into the water. To try and find him. The freezing cold water. Dark. Fast. Full of mud. I couldn't see him, my hands coming up empty time after time. And then his arm. Small. Cold. Little curled fist. I pulled him out.

But it was too late. I tried. I tried to shake the water out of him. But it was too late.

He was dead.

VICTORIA: –

Justine said you killed him.

CREATURE: I tried to give him to her, but she was looking at me, staring at me – and all I could see was hate.

VICTORIA: She thought you killed him.

CREATURE: So did you.

VICTORIA: –

CREATURE: –

VICTORIA: Why didn't you tell me? When you came to my house …

CREATURE: You were scared of me. When you thought I could kill. You were thinking about me.

VICTORIA: And you liked that?

CREATURE: At least it was something else. It wasn't hate.

Just for a moment.

VICTORIA doesn't have anything to say to this. CREATURE is looking at the cage.

CREATURE: Was he in pain?

VICTORIA: Yes.

CREATURE: So small.

Do you think it will hurt?

VICTORIA: It doesn't mean this will happen to you.

We don't know that.

CREATURE: I do.

CREATURE shows her his chest where the scars have all rotted into the flesh.

She comes closer to look at it.

VICTORIA: When did it start?

CREATURE: There's been a smell. And pain. For a long time.

At first, around scars. And then much deeper. Somewhere inside.

VICTORIA: Here…

She is about to help him sit down. But CREATURE doesn't fully trust her.

VICTORIA: Please.

He lets her help him. She helps him sit down. This comes as a relief.
Being able to sit down. And being helped by someone.

VICTORIA: There.

CREATURE: Does it disgust you?

VICTORIA: No, I don't mind.

CREATURE: I remember this room. It seemed bigger.
              Brighter.

              It was very *(he is looking for the right word)* …
              sharp.

              Now everything is cloudy. Soft.

VICTORIA: –

CREATURE: But it's still cold.

CREATURE is still.

VICTORIA: Would you like a blanket?

CREATURE: I don't know.

VICTORIA gets the cover from the bed and puts it over him.

CREATURE: Why did you do it?

VICTORIA: Do what?

CREATURE: Why did you make me?

VICTORIA: I wasn't going to. I wasn't going to make …
              anyone.

CREATURE: But I am here.

VICTORIA: I was hoping … I was trying to understand
              where life stops and death starts. To see if we
              can bring people back, if we can stop them
              from dying.

CREATURE: Why would you do that?

VICTORIA: Because it hurts too much. When they die.

VICTORIA looks at CREATURE.

CREATURE: You don't hate me.

VICTORIA: No, I don't.

CREATURE: It's always cold. All the time.

VICTORIA: I know.

CREATURE: I don't like it.

VICTORIA: I am sorry.

CREATURE: Is it going to happen soon?

VICTORIA: Yes. I think so.

CREATURE: –

Do you want me to go?

VICTORIA: –

No.

CREATURE: –

VICTORIA: No.

VICTORIA sits next to him.

CREATURE: If I tell you ... if I tell you what I remember.

VICTORIA: Yes?

CREATURE: Would that be useful? Would you learn
something, for the next time?

VICTORIA: Yes. I would.

CREATURE: So next time it might work.

VICTORIA wraps the blanket closer around him.

VICTORIA: Here.

She brings another one.

VICTORIA: Is that better?

CREATURE: No.

They both laugh. She sits next to him.

CREATURE: I don't remember much ... it was just cold.

VICTORIA: You don't have to do this.

CREATURE: I know.

        –

In the beginning it was cold and dark and quiet.

Then I heard a voice. She said 'hello'.

The End

CPSIA information can be obtained
at www.ICGtesting.com
Printed in the USA
LVHW010701020821
694270LV00012B/1415